S0-BMV-402

Animals in My World

WORKING ON THE FARM

Jefferson Madison
Regional Library
Charlottesville, Virginia

Jack Reader

HABA®

PowerKiDS
press™

NEW YORK

Published in 2018 by The Rosen Publishing Group, Inc.
29 East 21st Street, New York, NY 10010

Copyright © 2018 by The Rosen Publishing Group, Inc.

All rights reserved. No part of this book may be reproduced in any form without permission in writing from the publisher, except by a reviewer.

First Edition

Editor: Melissa Raé Shofner
Book Design: Michael Flynn

Photo Credits: Cover Conny Sjostrom/Shutterstock.com; pp. 5, 24 (tractor) linerpics/Shutterstock.com; p. 6 L.E.MORMILE/ Shutterstock.com; p. 9 Dennis Albert Richardson/Shutterstock.com; p. 10 bibiphoto/Shutterstock.com; p. 13 Berna Namoglu/Shutterstock.com; p. 14 thieury/Shutterstock.com; p. 17 Naruedom Yaempongsa/Shutterstock.com; p. 18 Poly Liss/Shutterstock.com; p. 21 gorillaimages/Shutterstock.com; p. 22 Serge Kozak/Corbis/Getty Images; p. 24 (eggs) kathayut kongmanee/Shutterstock.com; p. 24 (wool) francesco de marco/Shutterstock.com.

Cataloging-in-Publication Data

Names: Reader, Jack.
Title: Working on the farm / Jack Reader.
Description: New York : PowerKids Press, 2018. | Series: Animals in my world | Includes index.
Identifiers: ISBN 9781538321935 (pbk.) | ISBN 9781538321959 (library bound) | ISBN 9781538321942 (6 pack)
Subjects: LCSH: Working animals–Juvenile literature. | Farms–Juvenile literature.
Classification: LCC SF172.R43 2018 | DDC 591.5–dc23

Manufactured in China

CPSIA Compliance Information: Batch #BS17PK: For Further Information contact Rosen Publishing, New York, New York at 1-800-237-9932

Please visit: www.rosenpublishing.com and www.habausa.com

CONTENTS

In the Field

The farm is a busy place, and there's always work to do. The farmer uses a tractor. He moves the hay into the barn. The animals have work to do, too!

The horses work on the farm. They help the farmer. The horses are big. They're strong, too. They pull the cart. They plow the field.

The dog has a job on the farm. She watches the sheep. She keeps the sheep safe. The dog helps the farmer. She herds the sheep into their pen.

Things to Buy

There are cows on the farm. They have work to do. The cows make milk. The farmer milks the cows. People buy the milk from the farmer.

The sheep work on the farm. They grow wool coats. The farmer cuts the sheep's coats. He bags up all the wool. People buy the wool from the farmer.

There are chickens on the farm. They have a job to do. The chickens lay eggs. The farmer gathers the eggs. People buy the eggs from the farmer.

Helping Out

The cat has work to do. He catches mice. The cat chases mice in the barn. He chases mice in the field. The cat helps out on the farm.

The pigs help on the farm. They have work to do each day. The pigs eat the farmer's old food. They don't let the food go to waste.

The farmer's children work on the farm. They help the farmer. The children pick apples. They pick berries, too. People buy the fruit from the farmer.

The farmer's children brush the horses. They take the dog for walks. The children also feed the baby animals. Everyone works on the farm.

WORDS TO KNOW

eggs

tractor

wool

INDEX

Wrinkled pages 5-11-21 JJE/CR

WITHDRAWN
APR - - 2018